RABINDRANATH TAGORE

SONGS OF LOVE

MOHIT CHAKRABARTI

ATLANTIC PUBLISHERS AND DISTRIBUTORS

Published by
ATLANTIC PUBLISHERS AND DISTRIBUTORS
B-2, Vishal Enclave, New Delhi-27
Phone 5413460, 5429987

Sales Office
4346/4C, Ansari Road, Darya Ganj,
New Delhi-110 002
Phone 3273880, 3285873
Fax 91-11-3285873

ISBN 81-7156-394-5

Typeset at
APD Computer Graphics
B-2, Vishal Enclave, New Delhi-110 027
Printed in India at
Mehra Offset Press
New Delhi

DEDICATED
To

Dr. Minati Choudhury, R.G. Kar Medical College & Hospital, Calcutta

Shri Supriyo Tagore, Santiniketan

Dr. Somendranath Bandyopadhyay, Santiniketan

PREFACE

Love, the most serene component of human sensibility, is always unique. To Rabindranath Tagore, it has its more appealing and poignant efflorescence in multidimensional avenues.

Rabindranath Tagore: Songs of Love is a translation of a few selected love-songs of Tagore. These manifest love from diverse perspectives – love as a bond of union, reminiscence, introspection and light or as an eternal fountain of joy and hope, challenge and charm, buoyant thrill and beauty. Moreover, love also appreciates the endless power and glory of man who never yields to sorrows and sufferings, loss and pain, wounds and disappointments.

An unparalleled singer of human excellance, Rabindranath Tagore upholds love as the supreme force for the unison of man and the All Beautiful. Here is a Saint-Singer who sings the songs of the inner world of our hearts yawning for a re-tuning of consciousness in every direction.

Rabindranath Tagore: Songs of Love might serve as a constant companion to anyone who wants to be christened in the songs of love.

Mohit Chakrabarti

(1)

Āmār yete sare nā man –
Tomār duār pārāye ami yāi ye hārāye
Atal virahe nimagan.
Calite calite pathe sakali dekhi yena miche,
Nikhil bhuvan piche dāke anukṣan.
Āmar mane Kevali vāje
Tomāy kichu deoyā hala nā ye.
Yave cale yāi pade pade vādha pāi,
Phire phire asi akāraṇ.

My mind desires not to depart –
Crossing your door I lose myself
Immersed, as it were, in the unfathomable
sea of separation.
Trekking on the way, everything do I behold to be false,
Timeless does the wide world beckon behind.
All the time does my mind ache.
Ah, nothing did I offer you.
When I depart, I halt at every step
And return for reasons unknown.

(2)

Val, golāp, more val,
Tui phuṭivi sakhi, kave.
Phul phuṭeche Cāri pāś, cmad hāsiche sudhāhās,
Vāyu pheliche mṛdu śvās, pākhi gāiche madhurave –
Tui phuṭivi sakhi, kave.
Prāte paḍeche, śiśirkaṇā, sṃājhe vahiche dakhinā vāy,
Kāche phulavātā sāri sāri –
Dūre pātār ādāle sāṁājher tārā mukhāni dekhite cāy.
Vāye dūr hate āsiyāche, yata bhramar phiriche kāche,
Kaci kiśalayguli rayeche nayan tuli –
Tārā śudhāiche mili save,
Tui phuṭivi sakhī, kave.

Tell, Rose, tell me,
When you will bloom, my friend.
Everywhere the flowers bloom, the moon shines with her nectar smile
Softly does the wind breathe, sweetly are the birds singing,
When you will bloom, my friend.
Dew drops have fallen in the morn, the southern wind is blowing in the evening,
In rows are flowermaids nearby.
Yonder are the evening stars at the backdrop of leaves
Eager to behold thy countenance.
From a distance has the wind turned up
Countless bees are moving close,
Tender green leaves are with weeping eyes –
And they all ask together:
When will you bloom, my friend!

(3)

Gela go –
Phirila nā, cāhila nā, pāṣaṇ se.
Kathāṭio kahila nā, cale gelà go.
Nā yadi thākite cāy yāk yethā sādh yāy,
Ekelā āpan-mane din ki kāṭive nā.
Tai hok, hok tave–
Ār tāre sādhiva nā.

O she has gone
She neither turned nor did she look, like a rock she is.
If she wants not to stay, let her go where she wishes.
Won't the day pass in a lonely mind !
Let it be so, then let it be.
No more shall I request her.

(4)

Keha kāro man vujhenā kāche ese sare yāy.
Sohāger hāsiṭi kena cokher jale mare yāy.
Vātās yakhan keṁde gela prāṇ khale phul phaṭila nā,
Sāṁjher velā ekākinī kena re phul jhare yāy.
Mukher pāne ceye dekho, āṁkhite milāo āṁikhi –
Madhur prāṇer kathā prāṇete rekho nā ḍhāki.
E rajanī rahive nā, ār kathā haivo nā –
Prabhāṭe rahive śudha hṛdayer hāy-hāy.

None feels the mind of the other,
each comes nearer and departs.
Why does the smile of endearment die down in tears ?
When the wind wept away,
flowers bloomed not with heart wide open.
Why do they lonely wither away in the hours of evening?
Look at the face, unite eyes with eyes
Cover not the sweet words of the heart in your heart.
This night will bid farewell, no more will we speak.
The morning will mourn with the wailings of the heart.

(5)

Man jāne manomohan āila, man jāne sakhi !
Tāi keman kare āji amār prāṇe.
Tāri sourabh rahi vahila ki samīraṇ āmār pāraṇpane.

Mind knows the enchanter of mind did come,
O friend, my mind does know
And so how my heart throbs !
Does the air bring forth a-sweeping
the fragrance towards my heart ?

(6)

Sājāva tomāre hė phul diye diye,
Nānā dharaner vanaphul diye diye.
Āji vasantarāte pūrṇimācandrakare
Dakṣiṇapavane priye.
Sājāva tomāre he phul diye diye.

With flowers shall I adorn thee,
With flowers wild and multicoloured.
O dear, in this moonlit night of the spring
in the southern wind
With flowers shall I adorn thee.

(7)

Ye phul jhare sei to jhare, phul to thāke phuṭite
Vātās tāre uḍiye ne yāy, maṭi meśāy māṭite,
Gandha dile, hāsi dile, phuriye gela khelā.
Bhālovāsā diye gela, tāi ki helāphelā.

The flower that droops down is the lone flower
that withers,
Others go on ablooming.
The wind takes her afloating, the earth mingles her
with the soil.
Fragrance did she spread with laughter as well.
The play came to an end
Love did she leave behind, and so is this
difference an outcome.

(8)

Nayan mele dekhi āmạ̄y vāṁdhan veṁdheche.
Gopane ke eman kare e phāṁd pheṁdeche.
Vasantarajaniśeṣe vidāy nite gelem hese –
Yāvār velāy vaṁdhū āmāy kāṁdiye keṁdeche.

With eyes open do I behold that strings have
enwrapped me.
Who has planned such a trap in seclusion?
At the end of the spring-night I sought adieu in smile
At the time of her farewell, the bride has wept
by forcing me to weep.

(9)

Sakhī, se gela kothāy, tāre ḍeke niye āy.
Dāmḍāva ghire tāre tarutalāy.
Āji o madhue sāṁjhe kānane phuler mājhe
Hese hese leḍāve se, dekhiva tāy.
Ākāśe tārā phuṭeche, dakhinā vātās chuṭeche,
Pākhiṭi ghumaghore geye uṭheche.
Āy lo ānandamayī, madhur vasanta laye
Lāvaṇya phuṭāvi lo, tarutalāy.

Where did he depart, friend! Call on him.
Beneath the tree shall I stand encircling him.
In this pleasant evening today amid flowers
in the garden
He'll stroll with a smile, and that will I behold.
Stars have adorned the sky, towards the south
has the wind sped on,
In the realm of slumber has the bird sung out.
O the joyous, come with tunes of pleasing spring
To bloom smoothness beneath the tree.

(10)

Ke ḍāke! Āmi kabhu phire nāhi cāi.
Kata phul phuṭe aṭhe, kata phul yāy ṭuṭe,
Āmi śudhu vahe cale yāi.
Paraś pulakaras-bharā rekhe yāi, nāhi dii dharā.
Uḍe āse phulavās, latāpātā phele śvās,
Vane vane uṭhe hā-hutāś –
cakite śunite śudhu pāi – cale yai.
Āmi kabhu phire nāhi cāi.

Who harks? Never do I look back
So many flowers bloom, so many wither.
Alone do I sail along.
The touch brimmed with the fountain of joy
do I leave behind undisclosed
The fragrance of flowers flows aflying,
Creepers and leaves breathe
Wailings spring forth all thro' the forest
All of a sudden do I listen adieu !
Never do I look back.

(11)

Āmi hṛdayer kathā valite vyākul,
Sudhāilā na keha.
Se to ela nā, yāre sṁpilām
Ei prāṇ man deha.
Se ki mor tare path cāhe –
Se ki virahagīt gāhe
Yār vāṁśarīdhvani śuniye
Āmi tyjilām geha.

Eager am I to open out my heart
But none did ask me.
Ah, he to whom did I dedicate this life, mind and body,
Came not.
Does he wait wishing for me –
Does he sing the plaintive song –
He – ah, he for whom did I abandon my home
by listening to the sound of his flute.

(12)

Nimeṣer tare śarame vādhila, maramer kathā hala nā,
Janamer tare tāhāri lāgiye rahila maramavedanā,
Cokhe cokhe sadā rākhivāre sādh –
Palak paḍila, ghatila viṣād –
Melite nayan milāla svapan, emni premer ohalanā.

For a moment did shame prick me,
The words of the heart remained unspoken
The pains of the heart were left apart for him
throughout life.
The desire is to keep him all the time close to eyes.
The eyelids drooped, the agony did swoop –
The dream vanished with the opening of eyes.
Such is the trickery of love.

(13)

Āj yeman kare gāiche ākāś temni kare gāo go.
Yeman kare cāiche ākāś temni kare cāo go.
Āj hāoyā yeman pātāy pātāy marmariyā vanke kāṁdāy,
Temni āmār vaker mājhe kāmdiyā kāṁdāo go.

Tune on as the sky is singing today
Behold as the sky is looking on.
As the wind makes the forest weep by murmuring in leaves
Make me weep so by weeping amidst my heart.

(14)

Youvanasarasīnīre milanaśatadal
Kon cañoal vanyāy ṭalamal ṭalamal.
Śaramaraktarāge tār gopan svapna jāge,
Tāri gandhakeśar-mājhe
Ek vindu nayanajal
Dhīre vao dhīre vao, samīraṇ,
Savedan paraśan.
Śaṅkita citta mor pāche bhāne vrntaḍor –
Tāi akāraṇ karuṇāy mor āṁkhi kare chalāchal.

In the water of the stream of youth,
In what a turbulent flood
Dangling the lotuses of unison are !
With the blood red hue of shame
Her hidden dreams awaken.
Amid her perfumed hair
A single drop of tears adorns.
Slow slowly, O wind, slowly blow
With the touch of pain.
Fearful is my mind, lest the string of the twig does fall apart.
With pity unknown my eyes brim with tears.

(15)

Āmi keval tomār dāsi
Keman kare ānva mukhe 'tomāy bhālovāsi'.
Guṇ yadi mor thākta tave anek ādar milta bhave,
Vināmūlyer kenā āmi śricaranprayasi.

Only a maid-servant am I to you,
How can I utter 'I love you'?
If virtuous were I, much adoration would I receive
I *sans* any value seek shelter at your feet.

(16)

Vane eman phul phuṭeche
Mān kare thākā āj ki sāje.
Mān abhimān bhāsiye diye
Calo calo kuñjamājhe.
Āj kokile geyeche kuhu muhurmuhu,
Āj kānane oi vāṁsi vāje.
Mān kare thākā āj ki sāje.
Āj madhure miśāvi madhu, parāṇaṁdhu
Cāṃder āloy oi virāje.
Mān kare thākā āj ki sāje.

What a profuse blooming in the forest!
Is it fair to remain in pangs today?
Leaving all honour and prestige afloating
Let's go to the flower garden.
The cuckoo has time and again cooed today,
Yonder is the flute that plays on today.
Is it fair to remain in pangs today?
Let sweetness kiss sweetness today,
Yonder is the bride of the heart
adorned in the light of the moon.
Is it fair to remain in pangs today?

(17)

Vujhi velā vaye yāy,
Kānane āy torā āy.
Ālote phul uṭhla phuṭe, chāyāy jhare paḍe yāy.
Sādh chila re pariye deva – maner matan mālā geṁthe –
Kai se hala mālā gāṁthā, kai se ela hāy.
Yamunār ḍheu yācche vaye, velā cale yāy.

Time seems to sail on.
Come, ye come, to the flower garden.
Flowers came out ablooming in light, in shadow do they
wither away.
I wished I would adorn him with the garland made
as the mind wishes.
Where is the garland to be sewn, ah, where did he come –
The waves of the Yamuna roll on, time sails on.

(18)

Erā parke āpan kare, āpnāke par –
Vāhire vāṁśîr rave cheḍe yāy ghar.
Bhālovāse sukhe dukhe vyathā sahe hāsimukhe,
Maraṇere kare cirajīvananirbhar.

They endear others as their own, and make themselves alien.
With the sound of the flute outside, they leave the room,
With weal and woe do they love,
With smiling countenance do they forbear pain
And make death eternally dependent on life.

(19)

Vaṁdhu, tomāy karva rājā tarutale,
vanaphuler vinodmala deva gale.
Siṁhāsane vasaite hṛdaykhāni deva pete,
Abhiṣek karva tomāy āṁkhijale.

Beneath the tree shall I make thee king. O bride.
With the garland of entertainment made of forest flowers
Shall I adorn thee.
To make thee seated on the throne.
I shall stretch my heart.
With tears shall I felicitate thee.

(20)

Ekhano tāre cokhe dekhini, śudhu vāṁśi śunechi –
Man prāṇ yāhā chila diye phelechi.
Śunechi murati kālo tāre nā dekhāi bhālo.
Sakhī, valo āmi jal ānite yamunāy yāva ki.
Śudhu svapane esechila se, nayanakoṇe hesechila se.
Se avadhi sai, bhaye bhaye rai - āṁkhi melite bheve sārā hai,
Kānanapathe ye khuśî se yāy, kadamatale ye khuśî se cāy –
Sakhi, valo āmi āmkhi tule kāro pāne cāva ki.
Sakhi, āṁi amkhi tule kāro pāne cāva ki.

Not yet have I seen him with eyes, only the flute
have I heard to play on.
The mind or life whatsoever have I already surrendered.
His mien is black as I've heard, it's better not to see him.
Friend, tell me if to the Yamuna shall I go to bring water.

Only in dream did he come, in the corners of eyes
did he laugh.

From that time, friend, I remain in awe –
Lost am I in thought to open my eyes.
Whoe'er wills does tread on the way to the flower garden
Whoe'er wills does look at the feet of the *Kadam* tree
Friend, tell me if I with eyes raised
shall look at any one.
Friend, shall I look at anyone with eyes raised?

(21)

Āj tomāre dekhte elem anek diner pare.
Bhay karonā, sukhe thāko, vesîkṣaṇ thākva nāko –
Esechi daṇḍa-duyer tare.
Dekhva śudhā mukhkhāni, śunāo yadi śunva vāṇi,
Nāhay yāva āḍāl theke hāsi dekhe deśāntare.

After many a day did I come today to visit you.
Fear not, in happiness remain, not much shall I stay,
For a moment have I come.
Only the countenance shall I see, and listen to
the words, if you utter.
Or I shall traverse from land to land
by looking at your smile aside.

(22)

Jivane āj ki pratham ela vasanta !
Navinavāsanābhare hṛday keman kare,
Navin jivane hala jivanta.
Sukhabharā e dharāy man vāhirite cāy,
Kāhāre vasāte cāy hṛdaye.
Tāhāre khum̐jiva dik-diganta.

Is the spring come for the first time in life today?
With young desire ah, how the heart throbs !
The young in life becomes living.
In the world brimmed with happiness,
the mind wants to be exposed.
Whom does it want to be seated in the heart
All through shall I wander for her.

(23)

Yeyonā, yeyonā phire –
Dāṁḍāo vārek ḍāṁḍāo hṛday-āsane.
Cañcalasamirasama phiricha kena
Kusume kusume kānane kānane.
Tomāy dharite cāhi, dharite pāri ne –
Tumi gaṭhita yena svapane.
Eso he, tomāre vārek dekhi bhariye āṁkhi,
Dhariye rākhi yatane.
Prāṇer mājhe tomāre ḍhākiva,
Phuler pāśe vāṁdhiye rākhiva,
Tumi divasaniśi rahive miśi
Komal premaśayane.

Return not, go not back
Stand, stand for a while on the seat of the heart.

Like restless wind
Why do you tread on from flower to flower,
from one garden to the other?

I want to catch hold of you but I fail.
As if with dream you are framed
Come, O come, let me once see you with full eyes.
With care do I treasure you up.
Amid life shall I wrap you up
With flowers shall I entwine you
All thro' the day and the night
You will be in unison with the tender
bed of love.

(24)

Oi madhur mukh jāge mane.
Bhulivanā e jivane ki svapane ki jāgaraṇe:
    Tumi jāna vā nā jāna,
Mane sadā yena madhur vāṁśari vāje
    Hṛdaye sadā ācha vale.
Āmi prakāsite pāri ne,
    Śudhu cāhi kātar nayane.

That sweet countenance flashes in the mind.
In dreams or awakenings never shall I forget
                                        in this life.
Know ye or not
Let the sweet flute always play on in the mind
For you are always in the heart.
I fail to manifest myself
Only in plaintive eyes do I behold.

(25)

Premer phāṁd pātā bhuvane –
Ke kothā dharā paḍe ke jāne.
Garav sav hāy kakhan ṭuṭe yāy,
Salil vahe yāy nayane.
E sukhadharanite kevali cāha nite,
Jānanā have dite āpanā –
Sukher chāyā pheli kakhan yāve cali,
Varive sādh kari vedanā.
Kakhan vāje vāṁsi, garav yāy bhāsi –
Parān pade āsi vāṁdhane.

The trap of love is lain all thro' the world.
Who knows where one is trapped.
All the glory, alas, tears apart.
Eyes flow in tears
Only do you want to have in this happy earth,
Know ye not how to give yourself.
With the shadow of happiness will you leave unnoticed
Pain will you wilfully adore.
When the flute plays on, you know not,
Pride plies away.
In strings does life scramble.

(26)

Gharete bhramar ela gunguniye.
Āmāre kār kathā se yāy śuniye.
Ālote kon gagane mādhavi jāgla vane
Ela sei phul-jāgānor khavar niye.
Sārā din sei kathā se yāy śuniye.
Kemane rahi ghare, man ye keman kare –
Kemane kāṭe ye din din guniye.
Ki māyā dey vulāye, dila sav kāj bhulāye,
Velā yāy gāner sure jāl vuniye.
Amāre kār kathā se yāy śuniye

The bee came humming in the room.
Whose words does he convey to me?
In the light did he come with the message of the
flower-awakening news of the sky
Where *madhavi* blooms in the forest

All day long does he go on disseminating that news.

How can I remain in the room : Ah, how the mind aches,

How the day wanes counting on days
What a *maya* does he brush on,
And makes me forget all my work!
The day passes on weaving webs in tunes of music.
Whose words does he convey to me?

(27)

Divasarajani āmi yona kār
Āśāy āśāy thāki.
Tāi camakita man, cakita śravaṇ
Tṛṣita ākul āṁkhi.
Cañcal haye ghuriye veḍāi
Sadā mane hay yadi dekhā pāi,
'Ke āsiche vale camakiye cāi
Kānane dākile pākhi
Jāgaraṇe tāre nā dekhite pāi
Thāki svapaner āśe –
Ghumer āḍāle yadi dharā dey
Vāṃdhiva svapanapāśe.
Eta bhālovāsi eta yāre cāi
Mane hay nā to se ye kāche nāi,
Yena e vāsanā vyakul āvege
Tāhāre āsive dāki.

Day and night do I remain as if in the hope of
meeting some one I know not.
So the mind is startled, the ears alert,
the eyes thirsty and pining.
Restless do I roam about
All the time do I think if I could come across her.
I behold with a bizarre saying 'who is coming!'
As the birds beckon in the forest of flowers,
In waking I do not see her,
With the hope of dream do I await
Lest she is visible in the backdrop of slumber.
In the strings of dream shall I strip her.
So much do I love her, so much do I want her
close to me,
I think she is not away from me
As if this desire would call on her with
eager emotion.

(28)

Elem natun deśe –
Talāy gela bhagna tari, kule elem bhese.
Acin maner bhāṣā śonāve apurva kon āśā,
Vonāve rañin sutoy duhkhasukher jāl,
Vājve prāṇe natun gāner tāl –
Natun vedanāy phirva keṁde hese.
Nām-nā-jānā priyā
Nām-nā-jānā phuler mālā niyā hiyāy deve hiyā.
Youvaneri navocchvāse phāgun māse
Vājve nūpur ghāse ghāse.
Mātve dakhinvāy mañjarita lavañgalatāy,
Cañcalita elokeśe.

To a new country did I come –
The broken boat sank, to the bank did I come afloating.
What a unique hope the language of the mind unknown
would make me listen !

The web of weal and woe would be woven in coloured thread,
The resonance of new songs would ring.
With agony anew I would wander in laughter and tears.
The beloved whose name is yet to be known
Would adore heart with heart with the garland of
flowers unknown.

With the buoyant youth in the early spring
All thro' the grass bangles would ring
The southern wind would dance in the blooming
almond creepers
With restless dishavelled hair.

(29)

Ye din sakal mukul gela jhare
Āmāy dākle kena eman kare.
Yete have ye path veye śukno pātā āche cheye
Hāte āmār śunya dālā ki phul diye deva bhare.
Gānhārā mor hṛdaytale
Tomār vyakul vāṁśī ki ye vale
Nei āyojan, nei mama dhan, nei ābharaṇ, nei āvaraṇ –
Rikta vāhu ei to āmār vāṁdhve tomāy vāhuḍore.

Why did you call me so on the day
When all the flowers withered away?
Dry leaves cover the road to be trodden,
On my hand is the empty casket,
With what flowers would I fill it in?
Deep down in my songless heart
What a language your eager flute speaks!
No arrangement, nor do I have any wealth,
No ornament nor any coverings –
Only these arms of mine would entwine you around.

(30)

Ki sur vāje āmār prāne āmii jāni, mani jāne.
Kiser lāgi sadāi jāgi, kāhār kāche ki dhan māgi –
Tākāi kena pather pāne.
Dvārer pāśe prabhāt āse, sandhya name vaner vame,
Sakāl-sāṁjhe vāṁsi vāje, vikal kare sakal kāje –
Vājāy ke ye kiser tāne.

What a tune plays on in my heart!
Know I alone, the mind alone knows
Why I always remain awake,
What wealth do I beg, and to whom,
Why I look towards the way.
Beside the door does morning come,
Towards the left of the forest, evening droops down.
The flute plays on from morn till evening
And makes inactive in all work.
Ah, who plays it on and for what resonance!

(31)

Āmār ekṭi kathā vāṁśi jāne, vāṁsii jāne.
Bhare raila vaker talā, kāro kāche hay ni valā,
Keval vale gelem vāṁsîr kāne kāne.
Āmār cokhe ghum chilanā gabhir rāte
Ceye chilem ceye-thākā tārār sāthe.
Emni gela sārā rāti, pāi ni āmar jāgār sāthī –
Vāṁsîṭire jāgiye gelem gāne gāne.

The flute knows, the flute alone knows
a word of mine.
The depth of the breast remained in fulness.
None was informed
Only I whispered to the flute.
No sleep was there in my eyes at dead night.
With lookers on, stars did I remain a-seeing.
The whole night whiled away in such a way.
I did not have my waking partner –
With songs and songs did I make the flute awake.

(32)

Somay āmār nāi ye vāki,
Śeṣer prahar purṇa kare deve nā ki.
Vāre vāre kārā kare ānāgonā,
Kolāhale surṭuku ār yāy nā sonā –
Kṣaṇe kṣaṇe gāne āmār paḍe phāṁki.
Paṇ karechi, tomār hāte āpanāre
Seṣ kare āj cukiye deva ekevāre.
Miṭiye deva sakal khoṁjā, sakal vojhā,
Bhorvelākār eklā pathe calva sojā –
Tomār āloy duviye neva sajāg āṁkhi.

No more time is left for me.
Won't you fill in the last hours?
Who come and go again and again.
The tune is no longer heard amid noise
At times loopholes loom in my song.

I swear, in your hands
I'd totally submit myself today
I'd bring an end to all search, all burden.
At dawn towards the lonely path shall I tread on.
In your light shall I immerse my alert eyes.

(33)

Tumi āmāy dekechile chutir nimantraṇe,
Takhan chilem vahu dure kiser anveṣaṇe.
Kule yakhan elem phire takhan astaśikharśire
Cāila ravi śeś cāoyā tār kanakcāṁpār vane.
Āmār chuti phuriye geche kakhan anyamane.
Likhan tomār vinisutār śiuliphuler mālā,
Vāṇi ye tār sonār choṁyā aruṇ āloy ḍhālā –
Ela āmār klānta hāte phul-jhārano ṣiter rāte
Kuhelikāy manthar kon mouna samiraṇe.
Takhan chuti phuriye geche kakhan anyamane.

Thou hast called on me in the invitation of holidays.
I was then far away in search of the unknown.
When on the shore I came back, then, on the head
of the peak of setting
The sun made its last look in the forest of *kanakchampa*,
My holidays are over.
Know not I when in the absence of mind
The writings are entwined in the garland or *seuli* flowers
sans thread
Its message showered with the lustre of the sun
touched in gold
In my tired hands came in the flower-stripping night
of winter.
With what a silent wind indolent in the mirage
The holidays, then, are over unattended !

(34)

Dip nibe geche mama nisthasamire,
Dhire dhire ese tumi yeyo nā go phire.
E pathe yakhan yāve āṁdhāre cinite pāve –
Rajanigandhār gandha bhareche mandire.

Āmāre paḍive mane kakhan se lāgi
Prahare prahare āmi gān geye jāgi.
Bhay pāche śeṣ rate ghum āse āṁkhipāte,
Klānta kanthe mor sur phurāy yadi re.

My lamp is put out in the midnight wind.
O, go not back by coming gently
When you'll go back on this way
In darkness would you identify
The fragrance of *rajanigandha* has flooded the shrine.
When would you recall me for that
I remain awake in song from heart to heart
Lest in the last hours of night
Slumber seals my eyelids,
And my tune comes to a halt in my tired voice.

(35)

Āmi elem tāri dvare, dāk dilem andhakāre.
Āgal dhare dilem nāḍā – prahar gela pai ni sāḍā
Dekhte pelem nā ye tāre.
Tāre yāvār āge ekhān theke ei likhankhāni yava rekhe –
Dekhā tomār pāi vā nā pāi dekhte elem jeno go tāi,
Phire yāi sudurer pāre.

At her doors did I come, in darkness did I call on.
Holding on the bar, I gave a jolt –
Hours passed by, no response did I receive.

Ah, I failed to see her.
But ere I depart from this place
This letter did I leave behind:
No matter, if I meet you or not.
Know, o dear, that I came to see you.
Towards the shore of the endless do I go back.

(36)

Yakhan bhāṅla milan-melā
Bhevechilem bhulva nā ār cakṣer jal phelā.
Dine dine pather dhulāy mālā hate phul jhare yāy –
Janine to kakhan ela vismaraner vela.
Dine dine kaṭhin hala kakhan vuker tal –
Bhevechilem jharve nā ār āmār cokher jal.
Haṭhāt dekhā pather majhe, kānnā takhan thāme nā ye –
Bholār tale tale chila aśrujaler khelā.

When the banquet of union came to an end,
I thought I won't forget shedding tears any more.
Day by day in the dust of the path
flowers droop down from the garland.
I knew not when the hours of forgetting did come.
Day by day the labyrinth of the breast became
hard unnoticed.
I thought my tears would no longer roll on.
A sudden encounter on the way, weeping then
knows no break
In the backdrop of forgetting did the game of tears
go on.

(37)

Mane ki dvidhā rekhe cale cute se din bharā sāṁjhe,
Yete yete duyār hate ki bheve phirale mukhakhāni –
Ki kathā chila ye mane.
Tumi se ki hese gele āṁkhikoṇe –
Āmi vase vase bhāvi niye kampita hṛdayakhāni,
Tumi ācha dūr bhuvane.
Ākāśe uḍiche vakapāṁti
Vedanā āmār tāri sāthi.
Vārek tomāy śudhāvare cāi vidāykāle ki vala nāi,
Se ki raye gela go sikta yūthīr gandhavedane.

What a hesitation did you leave in the mind
on that day in the full-brimmed evening!
On your departure from the door
You turned away your thoughtful countenance.
What a word there was in your mind!
What a smile did you leave in the corner of the eyes
With a trembling heart I think a-sitting.
In the distant world you remain –
A young stork is flying in the sky.
The pains within me are her companion.
For once do I desire to ask you what you did not
say at the time of farewell :
Did it remain, o dear, in the pain adorned
in the fragrance of the drenched jasmine !

(38)

Din pare yāy din vasi pathapāśe
Gān pare gāi gān vasantavātāse.
Phurāte cāy nā velā tāi sur geṁthe khelā –
Rāgiṇir maricikā svapner ābhāse.
Din pare yāy din nāi tava dekhā,
Gān pare gāi gān rai vase ekā.
Sur theme yāy pāche tāi nāhi āsa kāche –
Bhālovāsā vyathā dey yāre bhālovāse.

Day after day passes, beside the way I sit,
Song after song do I sing in the wind of the spring.
The hours do not want to wane, and so is the game
by attuning –
The mirage of *ragini* is in the flickerings of dreams.

Day after day passes, no encounter with you takes place.
Song after song do I sing, alone do I remain seated.
Lest the tune comes to a halt, you do not come
nearer –
Love aches one whom one loves.

(39)

Kon gahan araṇe tāre elem hārāye
Kon dūr janamer kon smṛtivismṛtichāye.
Ai ālo-ādhāre
Kakhan vujhi dekhī, kakhan dekhi nā tāre –
Ken milansukher svapansāgar ela pārāye.
Dharā-adharār mājhe
Chāyānater rāgiṇite āmār vāṁsî vāje.
Vakul talār chāyār nācan phuler gandhe miśe
Jānine man pāgal kare kise.
Kon natinir ghūrṇi-āṃcal lāge āmār gāye.

In what a dense forest did I lose her!
In what a backdrop of reminiscence and oblivion
of long-lost life
In light and darkness today
Sometimes do I behold her sometimes not –
What a sea of dreams with the happiness of
unison did she come across.
Betwixt the existent and the non-existent
My flute plays on with the *ragini* of *chhayanat*.
The dancing of shadows at the *vakul* tree is in unison
with the fragrance of flowers
I know not what makes the mind mad
Which actress' whirling dress-end touches my body !

(40)

Prabhāt ālote mor kāṁdāye gele
Milanmālār dor chiṁḍiyā phele.
Pade yā rahila piche sav haye gela miche,
Vase āchi dūr-pāne nayan mele.
Eke eke dhuli hate kuḍāye mari
Ye phul vidāypathe paḍiche jhari.
Bhāvini rave nā leś se diner avaśeṣ –
Kāṭila phāgunvelā ki khelā khele.

Thou hast made my morning light weep.
Tearing off the string of the garland of union.
Whate'er is left behind has all become meaningless
With eyes feasting towards the distant
do I remain seated
One by one do I go on picking up from the dust
The flowers drooping down in the farewell path.
Never thought I that no trace of that day would last.
In what a game did I spend the hours of the early spring !

(41)

Viraha madhur hala āji madhurāte.
Gabhir ragiṇi uṭhe vāji vedanāte.
Bhari diyā pūrṇimāniśā adhir adarśantṛṣā
Ki karuṇ maricikā āne āṁkhipāte
Sudūrer sugandhadhārā vāyubhāre
Parāne āmār pathhārā ghure mare.
Kār vāṇi kon sure tāle marmare pallavajāle,
Vāje mama mañjirarāji sāthe sāthe

Languishment has become pleasant in the sweet tonight
A profound *ragini* tunes up in pain
Filling in with the night of the full moon
What a plaintive mirage does the restless thirst for
absence of union bring forth !
In the petals of eyes
With air adorned with nice streams of fragrance
from the distant
The lost wayfarer becomes weary in my heart.
Whose message murmurs in the nets of leaves
in tunes and rhythm unknown
And with it rings along my bunches of bangles !

(42)

Phirve nā tā jāni,
Āhā Tavu tomār path ceye jvaluk pradipkhāni
Gāṁthve nā mālā jāni mane,
Āhā Tavu dharuk mukul āmār vakulvane
Prāṇe Oi paraśer piyās āni.
Kothāy tumi path bholā,
Tavu Thāk na āmār duyar kholā.
Rātri āmār gitahinā,
Āhā Tavu Vāṁdhuk sure vāṁdhāk tomār vinā –
Tāre Ghire phiruk kāṅāl vāṇi.

Know I that you won't return.
Ah, let the lamp enkindle awaiting you.
In my mind do I know that you won't string the garland.
Ah, even then let the buds appear in my *vakul* forest
Bringing forth the thirst of that touch in the heart
where are you, the way-forgetful!
Yet let my doors remain open.
Nameless is my night.
Ah, let your *veena* be attuned.
Let the pining words wander around it.

(43)

Nilāñjañchāyā, prafulla kadamvavan,
Jamvupuñje śyām vananta, vanavithikā ghanasugandha.
Manthar nava nilanirad– parikirṇā diganta.
Citta mor panthāharā kāntavirahakāntāre.

The shadow of the cloud blue,
the *kadamva* forest cheerful,
The black end of the forest with clusters of blackberries,
the forest trees dense and with fair fragrance,
The horizon encompassed with cloud lazy, new and blue,
Waylost is my mind in the deep forest of endearing languishment.

(44)

Jvale ni ālo andhākāre
Dāo nā sārā ki tāi vāre vāre.
Tomār vāṁsî āmār vaje vuke kathin dukhe, gabhir sukhe –
Ye jāne nā path kāṁdāo tāre.
Ceye rai rāter ākāś-pāne
Man ye ki cāy tā mani jāne.
Asā jāge kena akāraṇe āmār mane kśaṇe kśaṇe,
Vyathār tāne tomāy ānve dvāre.

In darkness the light trimmed not
And so don't you respond again and again
In my heart your flute plays on in terrible sorrow
and happiness serene
You make one to whom the way is unknown, weep.
At the night sky do I gaze
The mind alone knows what it wants.
Why does hope aimlessly brew up at times in my mind
To bring you close to the door with the attraction of pain?

(45)

Dhūsar jivaner godhūlite klānta āloy mlānsmṛti.
Pūrṇa kari tāre miśāye giti.
Sei surer kāyā mor sāther sāthi, svapner saṅginī,
Tāri āveś lāge mane vasantavihval vane.
Dekhi tār virahī mūrti vehāger tāne
Sakaruṇ nata nayāne.
Pūrṇimā jyotsnāloke mile yāy
Jāgrata kokil-kākalite mor vāṁśīr gīte.

In the twilight of grey life the reminiscence fails
in the tired light
With the fusion of song do I fill it in.
The image of that tune is my companion, partner of dream.
Her aroma touches my mind in the spring-startled forest.
With the tune of *vehag* do I visualize
her languished image piteous and with drooping eyes.
The full moon is in unison with the flood of light,
With the cries of the waking cuckoos along with
the song of the flute.

(46)

Vane yadi phuṭla kusum,
Nei kena sei pākhi.
Kon sudūrer ākāś hate
Ānva tāre dāki?
Hāoyāy hāoyāy mātan jāge
Pātāy pātāy nācan lāge
Eman madhur gāner velāy
Sei sudhā ray vāki.
Udās-karā hṛdayaharā
Nā jāni kon dāke
Sāgarpārer vaner dhāre
Ke bhulāla tāke.
Āmār hethāy phāgun vṛthāy
Vāre vāre dāke ye tāy,
Eman rāter vyakul vyathāy
Kena se dey phāṁki.

When flowers bloomed in the forest
Why is that bird not there,
From which far away sky
Him shall I call in?
Intoxication spreads in the wind,
In the leaves dancing springs forth
In such a pleasant hour of music
He alone remains absent.
Know not I
With agonising and heart-stealing beckonings unknown
Who enticed him.
Beside the forest on the sea-shore.
My spring in vain beckons him time and again.
In anxious achings of such a night
Why does he fail to respond?

(47)

Tomār giti jāgālo smṛti nayan chalchaliyā,
Vādalaśeṣe karuṇ hese yena cāmeli kaliyā.
Sajal ghana megher chāye mṛdu suvās dila vichāye,
Nā-dekhā kon paraśaghāye paḍiche ṭalṭaliyā.
Tomār vāṇi-smaraṇkhāni āji vādalapavane
Niśithe vāripatan-sama dhvaniche mama śravaṇe.
Se vāṇi yena gānete lekhā diteche āṁki surer rekhā
Ye path diye tomāri priye, caraṇ gela caliyā.

The song of thine didst spring forth reminiscence
with eyes welled up in tears
Like the *chameli* bud at the end of rains
with a piteous smile.
In the shadow of the cloud watery and dense
the soft sweet fragrance spread o'er
With the stroke of the touch unseen and unknown
did it tumble down.
Thy message of reminiscence in the rainy wind of today
Like drops of rain at midnight rings in my ears.
That message written in the words of music
is drawing the lines of tunes –
On the way where, o beloved, the feet of thine
traversed on.

(48)

Sakaruṇ veṇu vājāye ke yāy videśî nāye,
Tāhari rāgiṇi lāgila gāye.
Se sur vāhiyā bhese āse kār sudūr virahavidhur hiyār
Ajānā vedanā, sāgarvelār adhir vāye
vaner chāye.
Tari gunjan lāgila gāye.
Tāi śune āji vijan pravāse hṛday mājhe
Saratśîśîre bhije bhairavi nirave vāje.
Chavi mane āse ālote o gite – yena janahin nadipathṭite
Ke caleche jale kalas bharite alas pāye
Vaner chāye.
Tāhāri ābhās lāgilā gāye.

Who goes playing on the plaintive flute in a foreign boat?
That very tune touched me.
Plying on that tune whose pain unknown of the languished heart
from a long distance comes afloating?
In the restless wind under the shadow of the forest!
That very resonance touched me.
Hearing that today amid the heart in the lonely life
abroad
The drenched *bhairavi* silently tunes on
in the early autum-dew.
The picture flashes on in the light and in music.
Who treads on along the river-path
With idle steps to fill in the pitcher with water
Beneath the shadow of the forest?
That very aroma touched me.

(49)

Kena nayan āpni bhese yāy jale.
Kena man kena eman kare.
Yena sahasā ki kathā mane paḍe –
Mane paḍe nā go tavu mane paḍe.
Cāri dike sav madhur nirav,
Kena āmāri parān keṁde mare.
Kena man kena eman kena re.
Yena Kāhār vacan diyeche vedan,
Yena Ke phire giyeche anādare –
Vaje Tāri ayatan prāṇer pare.
Yena sahasā ki kathā mane paḍe –
Mane paḍe nā go tavu mane paḍe.

Why the eye itself is flooded in water
Why the mind so quirers
As if all of a sudden what a word is recalled
No recalling o dear, and yet I recall
All around everything is pleasantly silent
Why the life of mine pines in crying
Why, why the mind so quivers
As if whose words have pained me
As if someone has gone back uncared
That very absence of care does ring in the heart
As if all of a sudden what a word is recalled
No recalling o dear, and yet I recall.

(50)

Tār hāte chila hāsir phuler hār katū raṅe raṇ-karā.
Mor sāthe chila dukher phaler bhār aśrur rase bharā.
Sahasā āsila, kahila se sundari 'Eso-na vadal kari'.
Mukhpāne tār cāhilām, mari mari, nidayā se manoharā.
Se laila mor bharā vādaler dālā, cāhila sakoutuke.
Āmi laye tār nava phāguner mālā tuliyā dharinu vuke.
'Mor hala jay' yete yete kay hese, dūre cale gela tvara.
Sandhyāy dekhi tapta diner śeṣe phulguli sav jharā.

On her hands was the garland of the flowers of smile
Adorned with countless colour.
With me was the burden of the fruit of sorrow
Filled in the juice of tears.
All of a sudden that beautiful maiden came and said,
'Do please come, let's exchange.'
I looked at her face. What a beauty!
She is unkind but lovely.
My offerings of full-flooded rains did she accept,
Curiously she looked.
Taking her garland of the new early spring
I clasped it on the breast.
'Victory to me!' said she with a smile while going.
Humbly did she depart.
In the evening did I see at the end of the hot day
The flowers all withered.

(51)

Hāy go, vyathāy kathā yāy duve yāy, yāy go –
sur hārālem aśrudhāre.
Tāri tomār sāgarnire, āmi phiri tire tire,
Thāṁi hala nā tomār sonār nāy go –
Path kothā pāi andhakāre.

Hāy go, nayan āmār mare durāśāy go,
ceye thāki dāṃḍiye dvāre.
Ye ghare oi pradip jvale tār thikānā keu nā vale,
Vase thāki pather nirālāy go
Cira-rāter pāthar-pāre.

Ah, with pain do my words sink, sink down.
In the flow of tears did I lose the tune.
Your boat is on the water of the sea,
On the shores do I roam about.
Ah, no room for me in the golden boat of yours
Where do I find the way in darkness?

Ah, in desparation do my eyes pine away
Towards the door do I stand and go on seeing.
None tells me about the room where that lamp burns.
Alone do I remain seated on the way
On the sea-shore of the eternal night.

(52)

Bharā thāk smṛtisudhāy vidāyer pātrakhāni.
Milaner utsave tāy phirāye diye āni.
Vīṣāder aśrujale nīraver marmatale
Gopane uṭhuk phale hṛdayer nūtan vāṇi.
Ye pathe yete have se pathe tumi ekā –
Nayane āṁdhār rave, dheyāne ālokrekhā.
Sārā din saṁgopane sudhāras dhālve mane
Parāner padmavane viraher viṇāpāṇi.

Let the cup of union be filled in with the wine of reminiscence,
Give me that back by bringing on the festival of union.
In tears of agony, in the core of silence,
Let the new message of the heart be in secret effulgence,
Alone you are on the way to be trekked.
Darkness will prevail in eyes, the line of light in meditation
All the day the pleasant wine will you pour in the mind
In the lotus land of life the goddess of languishment does adore.

(53)

Āmi ye gān gāi jāni ne se kār uddeśe.
Yave jāge mane akāraṇe cancal hāoyāy pravāsi pākhi –
Yena yāy sur bheṣe kūr uddeśe.
Oi mukhpāne ceye dekhi –
Tumi se ki atit kāler svapna
Ele nūtan kāler veśe.
Kabhu jāge mane ājo ye āse ni o jivane
Gāner kheyā se māge āmār tire ese, kār uddeśe.

Know not I for whom do I sing a song –
When with reasons unknown it springs forth in the mind
Like an alien bird in the restless air
As if the tune floats on to someone I know not.
Looking at that face do I behold
Ah, you are like a dream of yore,
In a new garb did you come.
Sometimes the mind recalls, not even today
did he come in my life.
The singing boat does he beg me ashore, for whom
I know not.

(54)

Āmār āpan gān āṃār agocare āmār man haraṇ kare,
Niye yāy se bhāsāye sakal simāri pāre.
Oi ye dūre kūle kūle phālgun ucchvasita phule phule –
Sethā hate āse duranta hāoyā, lāge āmār pāle.
Kothāy tumi mama ajānā sāthi,
Kāṭāo vijane viraharāti,
Eso eso udhāo pather yātri –
Tari āmār ṭalamal bharā yoyāre.

The song of my own steals my mind behind my sight
And takes me afloating beyond all endings
Yonder on the shores the early spring is in glamour
with flowers,
Turbulent wind blows from there and touches my sail.
Where do you, my unknown companion,
Spend the night of languishment in loneliness?
Come, come, o traveller of the vanishing path.
Dangling is my boat in spring tide.

(55)

Vāṇi mor nāhi.
Stavdha hṛday vichāyā cāhite śudhu jāni.
Āmi amāvibhāvari ālohārā,
Meliyā agaṇya tārā
Niṣphal āśāy niḥśeṣ path cāhi.
Tumi yāve vājāo vāṁśi sur āse bhāsi
Niravatār gabhire vihval vāye
Nidrāsamudra pārāye.
Tomāri surer pratidhvani tomāre dii phirāye,
Ke jāne se ki paśe tava svapner tire
Vipul andhakār vāhi.

No words have I
Know I only to took spreading the silent heart.
Darkest night am I *sans* light
Spreading countless stars,
In vain hope do I await endless path.
When you play on the flute, tunes afloat.
In the depth of silence in the perplexed wind
Crossing o'er the sea of slumber
The echo of your own tune do I give you back.
Who knows if it reaches the shore of your dream
Floating o'er darkness unending.

(56)

Ei udāsi haoyār pathe pathe mukulguli jhare;
Āmi kuḍiye niechi, tomār caraṇe diyechi
Laho laho karuṇ kare.
Yakhan yāva cale orā phuṭve tomār kole
Tomār mālā gāṁthar aṇulguli madhur vedanbhare
Yena āmāy smaraṇ kare.
Vou-kathā-kao tandrāhārā viphal vyathāy dāk diye hāy sārā
Āji vibhor rāte.
Dujaner kānākāni kathā dujaner milanavihvalatā,
Jyotsnādhārāy yāy bhese yāy doler pūrṇimāte.
Ei ābhāsguli paḍve mālāy gāṁtha kālke diner tare
Tomār alas dviprahare.

All thro' the way the buds wither in this eccentric wind.
Plucked have I these and placed at your feet.
Take, take on the piteous palm.
When I would depart
On your lap would they bloom.
Let your fingers that prepare garlands
Recall me with pleasant pain
Lost in drowsiness is *bou-katha-kao*, with pain
In vain does it baffle in beckonings
At this intoxicated night
The whisperings of the twain, the perplexing mood of the twain
Float on and on in floodlight on the full-moon spring-night.
These aroma would leave stamps on the garland strung tomorrow
In your idle noontime.

(57)

Āmi tomāri saṅge veṁdhechi āmār prān surer vāṁdhane
Tumi jāna nā, āmi peyeechi tomāre ajānā sādhane.
Se sādhanāy miśiyā yāy vakulagandha,
Se sādhanāy miliyā yāy kavir chanda –
Tumi jāna nā, ḍheke rekhechi tomār nām
Raṅin ōhāyār ācchādane.
Tomār arūp mūrtikhani
Phālguner ālote vasāi āni.
Vāṁśari vājāi lalit vasante, sudūr digante.
Sonār ābhāy kāṁpe tava uttari
Gāner tāner se unmādane.

My life have I entwined with thee in the string of tunes.
Know ye not, in meditation unknown do I have thee.
The perfume of *vakul* is in unison with that meditation
The rhymes of the poet synchronize with that meditation.
Know ye not, I've covered thy name with the coverings
of colourful shade.
Thy beautiful image
Do I place in the light of the early spring.
In the pleasing spring do I play on the flute
in the distant horizon.
With golden light does thy dress-end tremble
In that intoxication of the rhyme of the song.

(58)

Tumi kon bhāṅaner pathe ele suptarāte.
Āmār bhāṅla yā tā dhanya hala caraṇapāte.
Āmi rākhva geṁthe tāre raktamanir hāre,
Vakṣe dulive gapone nibhṛta vedanāte.
Tumi kole niyechile setār, miḍ dile niṣṭhur kare –
Chinna yave hala tār phele gele bhūmi-'pare.
Nirav tāhāri gān āmi tāi jāni tomāri dān –
Phere se phāgun hāoyāy hāoyāy surhārā mūrchanāte.

In which break-away path did you come at night asleep
Whate'er mine is broken with your footprint became blessed
I'd keep it in strings in the necklace of the gem of blood,
In desolate pain would it secretly swing on the breast.

On the lap did you take up the sitar,
Cruelly did you pull its strings.
When the strings tore apart,
On the ground did you leave it.
Silent is its music,
Know I that it's your gift.
With tuneless agonies does it move in the wind
of the early spring.

(59)

Ajānā sur ke diye yāy kāne kāne.
Bhāvnā āmār yāy bhese yāy gāne gāne.
Vismṛta janmer chāyāloke hāriye-yāoyā viṇār śoke
Phāgun hāoyāy keṁde phire pathahārā rāgiṇi.
Kon vasanter milanrāte tārār pāne
Bhāvnā āmār yāy bhese yāy gāne gāne.

Who whispers the tune unknown in ears?
In songs and songs my thoughts go on floating.
In the land of the shadow of forgotten birth
In the bereavement of the lost *veena*
The way-lost *ragini* wanders weeping in the wind
of the early spring
In which night of union of the spring towards the stars
My thoughts trek afloating in songs and songs.

(60)

Dekonā āmāre dekonā – deko nā.
Cale ye eseche mane tāre rekho nā.
Āmār vedanā āmi niye esechi,
Mūlya nāhi cāi ye bhālo vesechi.
Kṛopakaṇā diye ākṃkhi koṇe phire dekho nā.
Āmār duḥkha-yoyārer jalasrote.
Niye yāve more sav lāñchanā hate.
Dūre yāva yave sare takhan cinive more –
Avahelā tava chalanā diye ḍheko nā

Call on me not, don't call on.
Recall not one who has come back.
The pain of mine have I brought along.
No worth do I like to have for my love.
Don't look back in pity with the corners of eyes.
My sorrow is in unison with the current of the
spring tide.
From all sufferings, would it take me away.
When away shall I move you'll then know me.
Cover not the neglect of yours with trickeries.

(61)

Duḥkha diye meṭāva duḥkha tomār,
Snān karāva atal jale vipul vedanār.
Mor saṁsār diva ye jvāli, śodhan have e moher kāli,
Maraṇvyathā diva tomār carane upahār.

With sorrow shall I appease your sorrow.
In the deep water of the sea of pain
shall I bathe.
I shall lit up the world of mine,
this darkness of dissipation would then be purified.
At your feet shall I place the pain of death as my gift.

(62)

Vājive sakhi vāṁsî vājive –
Hṛdayarāj hṛde rājive.
Vacan rāśî rāśi kothā ye yāve bhāsi,
Ādhāre lāja hāsi sājive.
Nayane āṁkhijal karive chalāchal
Sukhavedanā mane vājive.
Marame murachiyā milāte cāve hiyā
Sei caraṇayugarājive.

The flute will play on, friend, on the flute will play.
The king of the heart would adorn the heart.
Countless words will float towards the unknown.
The bashful smile will adorn on the lips.
Tears will well up in brightness,
The pangs of happiness will ring in the mind.
Fainting in shame, the heart will want to
be in unison
With those twain feet.

(63)

Sakhā he, ki diye āmi tusiva tomāy
Jarjar hṛday āmār marmavedanāy,
Divāniśi aśru jhariche sethāy.
Tomār mukhe sukher hāsi āmi bhālovāsi –
Abhāginir kāche pāche se hāsi lukāy.

O friend, with what shall I please thee!
My heart is strewn with the pangs of pain.
Day and night tears fall there.
The smile of happiness do I love in thy face,
Lest to a luckless maiden that smile conceals.

(64)

Kholo kholo dvār, rākhiyo nā ār
vāhire āmāy dāṁdāye.
Dāo sādā dāo, ei dike cāo,
Eso dui vāhu vāḍāye.
Kāj haye geche sārā uṭheche sandhyātārā.
Āloker kheyā haye gela deyā
Astasāgar pārāye.
Bhari laye jhāri enecha ki vāri,
Sejecha ki śuci dukūle.
Veṁdhecha ki cul, tulecha ki phul,
Geṁthecha ki mālā mukule.
Dhenu ela goṭhe phire, pākhirā eseche niḍe,
Path chila yata juḍiya jagata
Āṁdhāre giyeche hārāye.

Come, open the door,
Keep me no more standing outside.
Respond, respond please.
Look this way,
Come, stretch the two arms.
The work is over.
Up is the evening star.
The sailing of light
Has already crossed the setting sun.
With baskets filled in
Have you brought water,
Have you purified yourself on the two shores,
Have you trimmed your hair, plucked flowers
And prepared garlands with flowers?
To the cowshed the cows came back,
To the nests the birds returned.
All the paths whatsoe'er
Are lost in the darkness amid the world.

(65)

Tomār maner ekṭi kathā āmāy valo.
Tomār nayan kena eman chalachala.
Vaner 'pare vṛṣti jhare jhara jhara rave.
Sandhyā mukharita jhillisvare nipakuñjatale.
Śāler vithikāy vāri vahe yāy kalakala.
Āji digantasimā
Vṛṣti-āḍāle hārāla nilimā –
Chāyā paḍe tava mukher 'pare,
Chāyā ghanāy tava mane mane kṣaṇe kṣaṇe,
Aśrumanthar vātāse vātāse tomār hṛday ṭālaṭala.

Tell me a single word of your mind
Why your eyes are welled up in tears.
Rains fall in the forest with a dripping sound
With the sound of the crickets the evening is agog
beneath the garden of *kadamva*.

In the *sal* trees, water flows on in a murmuring voice.
The horizon today
Loses the sky at the backdrop of rains.
Yet the shadow falls on the face.
Shadow at times consolidates in every mind.
Trembling is your heart with the wind
burdened with tears.

(66)

Godhūlilagane meghe ḍhekechila tārā.
Āmār yā kathā chila haye gela sārā.
Hayto se tumi sona nāi, sahaje vidāy dile tāi–
Ākās mukhar chila ye takhan, jharajhara vāridhārā.
Ceyechinu yave mukhe tola nāi āṁkhi
Āṁdhāre nirav vyathā diyechila ḍhāki.
Ār ki kakhano kave oman sandhyā have –
Janamer mato hāy haye gela hārā.

In the twilight hour stars were covered with the cloud
Whate'er I wanted to say was over.
Perhaps you heard that not, and so you easily
bid me adieu.
Then was the sky enamoured, rains dripping.
When I looked at your face, you raised not your eyes.
Silent pain was wrapped up in darkness.
Will there ever be such an evening, and when?
Lost it is for ever like life, ah!

(67)

Meghachāye sajal vāye man āmār
Utalā kare sārāvela kār lupta hāsi, supta vedanā hāy re.
Kon vasanter niśîthe ye vakulmālākhāni parāle
Tār dalguli geche jhare, śudhu gandha bhāse prāṇe.
Jāni phirive nā ār phirive nā, jāni tava path geche sudūre.
Pārile nā tavu pārile nā ciraśūnya karite bhuvan mama-
Tumi niye gecha mor vāṁsîkhāni, diye gecha tomār gān.

In the shadow of cloud and in the drenched wind
My mind revives the lost smile, the pain inherent,
ah, all the time.
The petals of *vakul* garland that you adorned me
at spring midnight
Are withered away, the fragrance alone floats on in the
heart.
Know I that you won't return, will no more return,
Know I that your path is far away,
No, you succeeded not in making my world eternally vacant.
My flute have you taken away, and you've left for me your
songs.

(68)

Varṣanmandrita andhakārā esechi tomāri e dvāre,
Pathikere laho ḍāki tava mandirer ek dhāre.
Vanapath hate sundari, enechi mallikāmañjari –
Tumi lave nij veṇivandhe mane rekhechi e durāśāre.
Kono katha nahi vale dhire dhire phire yāva cale.
Jhillijaṁkṛta niśīthe pathe yete vāṁśarite
Śeṣ gān pathava tomā-pāne śeṣ upahāre.

In darkness agog in rains have I come to this
door of yours.
Call the traveller in beside your temple.
O dear, from the forest path have I brought
the bunch of *mallika*.
On the tuft of hair would you place –
this hopeless hope do I cherish.
Slowly would I depart *sans* saying a single word –
In the gift finale shall I send my song to you.

(69)

Āmi tomār preme hava savār kalaṇkabhāgi.
Āmi sakal dāge hava dāgi.
Tomār pather kāṁṭā karva chayan, yethā tomār dhulār śayan.
Sethā āṁcal pātva āmār – tomār rage anurāgi.
Āmi śuci-āsan tene tene veḍāva nā vidhān mene,
Ye pāṅke oi caraṇ paḍe tāhāri chāp vakṣe māgi.

With thy love shall I be a sharer of the blemishes of all.
With all scars shall I be marked.
The thorns of thy path where thy dust sleeps, shall I
pick-up.
My dress-ends shall I spread there, devoted am I
to your arrogance
Pulling on the purified seat I won't roam about
in strictures.
I pray for the footprints on the breast, that fall on
the mud.

(70)

Eso āmār ghare.
Vāhir haye eso tumi ye ācha antare.
Svapanduyār khule eso aruṇ āloke
Mugdha e cokhe.
Kṣaṇakāler ābhās hate cirakāler tare eso āmār ghare.
Duḥkhasukher dole eso, prāṇer hillole eso.
Chile āśār arūp vāni phāgunavātāse
Vaner ākul niśvāse –
Evār phuler praphulla rūp eso vuker 'pare.

Come to my room,
Come out ye who is in the heart.
Come in sunshine opening the doors of dream
with these enamoured eyes
Come for ever in my room, from the aura of
time transcient
Come with the swing of sorrow and happiness
Come with the thrill of life.
Like a serene language of hope in the wind
of the early spring
You were in the pining breath of the forest.
Come now with the pleasing look of flowers
on my breast.

(71)

Tomār gopan kathāṭi sakhi, rekho nā mane.
Śudhā āmāy, volo āmāy gopane.
Ogo dhiramadhurahāsini, volo dhiramadhura bhāṣe –
Āmi kāne nā śuniva go, śuniva prāṇer śravaṇe.
Yave gabhir yāmini, yave nirav medini,
Yave suptimagan vihaganiḍ kusumākanane,
Volo aśrujaḍita kanṭhe, volo kampita smita hāse –
Volo madhuravedanavidhura hṛdaya śaramanamita nayane.

Friend, don't keep it close in mind – your secret words
Tell me, tell me alone in confidence.
O with eyes pleasing and soft, tell me with
the speech soft and sweet
O with ears I won't hear, I would listen
with the ears of the heart.
In the night serene, in the silent world,
On the sleeping-nests of the garden of flowers

Tell with a tearful voice
Tell with a trembling smile
Tell with a heart pleasing and agonising
in eyes drooped down in shame.

(72)

Tumi rave nirave hṛdaye mama
Niviḍa nibhṛta pūrṇimānisîthini-sama.
Mama jivana youvana mama akhila bhuvana
Tumi bharive gourave nisithini-sama.
Jāgive ekāki tava karunā āṁkhi,
Tava ancalachāyā more rahive ḍhāki.
Mama duḥkhavedana mama saphala svapana
Tumi bharive sourabhe nisîthini-sama.

In silence will you remain in the heart
Like the full-moon midnight silent and serene
My life and youth, my unending world
Like midnight would you fill in glory.
Alone would your plaintive eyes awake
The shadow of your dress-end would cover me up.
My pains of sorrow, my dream unsuccessful
Like midnight would you fill in fragrance.

(73)

Āmi cini go cini tomāre ogo videśini.
Tumi thāka sindhupāre ogo videśini.
Tomāy dekhechi śāradaprāte, tomāy dekhechi mādhavi rāte,
Tomāy dekhechi hrdi-majhare ogo videsini.
Āmi ākāśe pātiyā kān śunechi śunechi tomāri gān,
Āmi tomāre saṁpechi prāṇ ogo videśini.
Bhuvan bhramiyā śeṣe āmi esechi nūtan deśe
Āmi atithi tomāri dvāre ogo videśini.

Know I, o foreigner, I know you
On the shores of the sea is your abode.
In the autumn morning and at the *madhavi* night
have I seen you,
In the core of my heart, o foreigner, have I seen you.
Placing my ears in the sky have I listened
to your song
I've submitted my life to you, o foreigner.
After trekking the world to a new land
have I come at last
A guest am I at your doorstep, o foreigner.

(74)

Āmi ye ār saite pāri ne.
Sure vāje maner mājhe go, kathā diye kaite pāri ne.
Hṛdaylatā nuye paḍe vyathābharā phuler bhāre go,
Āmi se ār vaite pāri ne.
Āji āmār niviḍ antare
Ki hāoyāte kāṁpiye dila go pulak-lāgā ākul marmare.
Kon guni āj udās prāte miḍ diyeche kon viṇāte go –
Ghare ye ār raite pāri ne.

No more can I forbear.
O, tune aches in the mind I fail to express in words
Down bends the creeperlike heart with the burden of
painful flowers.
No more can I bear that.
In my serene heart today
O, what a wind trembled is joyous and restless murmurings!
On this eccentric morning who is the expert
that has attuned the *veena* unknown:
No more shall I remain in the room.

(75)

Hāy re, ore yāy nā ki jānā,
Nayan ore khuṁje veḍāy, pāy nā ṭhikānā –
Alakh pathei yāoyā āsā, śuni caraṇdhvanir bhāsā-
Gandhe śudhu hāoyāy hāoyāy raila niśānā.

Kemaṇ kare jānāi tāre
Vase āchi pather dhāre.
Prāṇe ela sandhyāvelā āloy chāyāy raṅin khelā –
Jhare-paḍā vakul ḍāle vichāy vichānā.

Ah, can't she be known?
The eyes seek her but find her not anywhere.
In the way unmarked does she come and go,
The language of the sounds of feet do I listen,
In frangrance alone in the wind did the
direction remain.

How can I inform her
That the way beside am I remain seated ?
At dusk came in the heart the coloured play
in light and shade –
The bed is strewn with the withered cluster of *vakul*.

❀

INDEX OF FIRST WORDS